LOOK AT
HAIR

Franklin Watts
12A Golden Square
London W1R 4AB

Franklin Watts Australia
14 Mars Road
Lane Cove
N.S.W. 2066

ISBN 0 86313 568 4

Design: David Bennett
Illustrations: Julia Osorno

Printed in Italy by G. Canale & C. S.p.A. Turin

The author and publisher would
like to thank the following people
for their participation in the
photography for this book:
Jessica Ratner, Arthur Jeffes, Lucy
Chapman, Coco Ndekekede, Yukari Sato,
Carly Martin, William Perry, Chloe
Thomson, Kate Tatum, Ursula Hageli
of the Royal Ballet, Leo Thomson,
Garry Studd,

Additional photographs:
Alan International School of
Hairdressing: page 10 (right);
Chris Fairclough: page 10 (left);
Sally and Richard Greenhill: pages 15, 16, 17;
Hutchinson Library: pages 7 (right), 13;
Richard Olivier, Select:
pages 14 (left), 18 (right and left);
Rex Features Ltd: pages 14 (right), 28;
Science Photos: page 9;
John Watney: page 22;
Zefa: pages 7 (left), 8, 10 (top right),
19, 21 (left and right), 25, 28

LOOK AT
HAIR

Ruth Thomson
Photography by Mike Galletly

FRANKLIN WATTS

London · New York · Sydney · Toronto

How different hair can be!
What is yours like?

Straight, wavy or crinkly?
Blonde, brown, red or black?
Short, shoulder length or long?

Babies are usually born
with very little, fine hair.
As they grow, their hair
becomes longer and thicker.
Sometimes it changes colour.

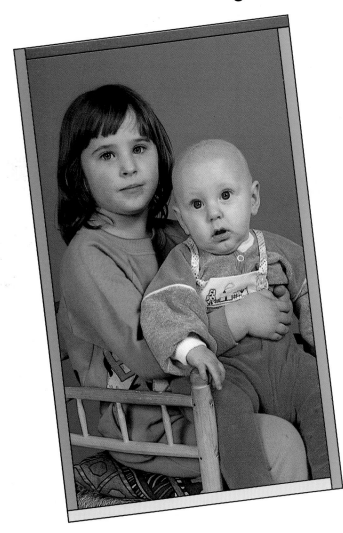

Hair grows all the time.
If you never cut it,
it would grow down to your waist
and eventually to your feet!

When people grow old,
their hair grows more slowly
and often turns white.
Some men lose most of their hair.
They become bald.

These are magnified strands
of hair.
Can you see how rough and scaly
they are?

Hair is one of the few parts
of the body that you can change
very easily.
It can be cut, dyed, curled,
straightened, tinted with colour ...

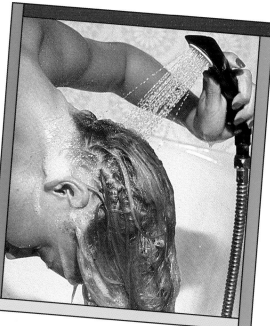

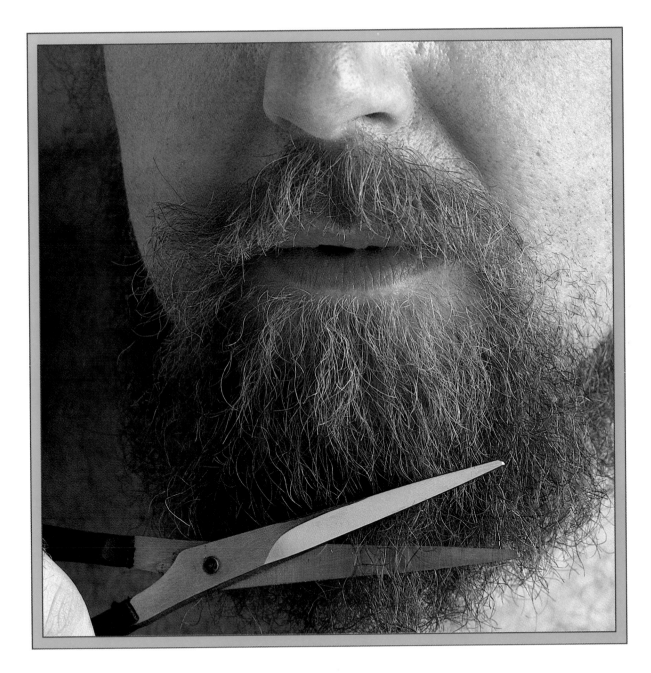

and trimmed into shape.

By changing your hairstyle,
you can change the way you look.

Hairstyles can be very simple
or quite elaborate, like this one.

Sometimes people choose
a particular hairstyle to show
they are part of a certain group.

Hippies had very long hair.
Skinheads have very short hair.

Punks have very spiky hair.

The way that some people treat their hair shows
that they are followers of a certain religion.

Buddhist monks keep their heads
completely shaven.
This shows their humility.

Rastafarians never cut their hair.
This shows their respect for God

Sikhs leave their hair uncut too, but they cover it with a turban.

Christian nuns always cover their hair. Some of them shave their heads.

Greek Orthodox priests have both
long hair and long beards.
They are the only men in Greece
who wear beards.

Some people have to wear their hair in a particular way for their work.

Ballet dancers pin their hair up
so that they don't get dizzy
when they spin round and round.

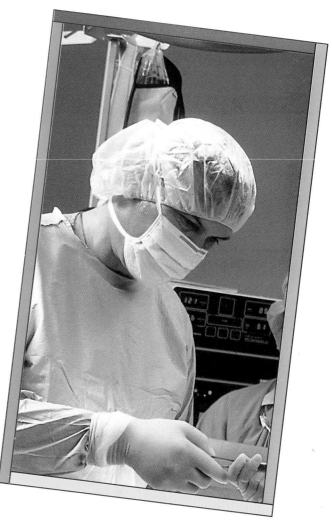

Why do you think surgeons
and cooks cover their hair
with caps like these?

21

Actors often need to change their looks.
Wigs, false beards and moustaches are useful disguises.

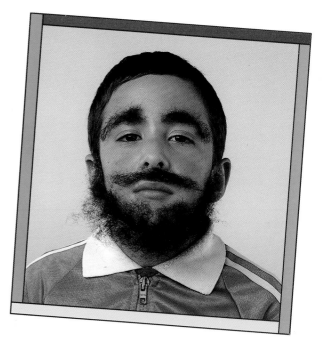

See for yourself.
Draw ten identical faces
How different can you make them
look by adding hair, eyebrows
and a beard or a moustache?

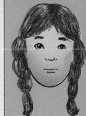

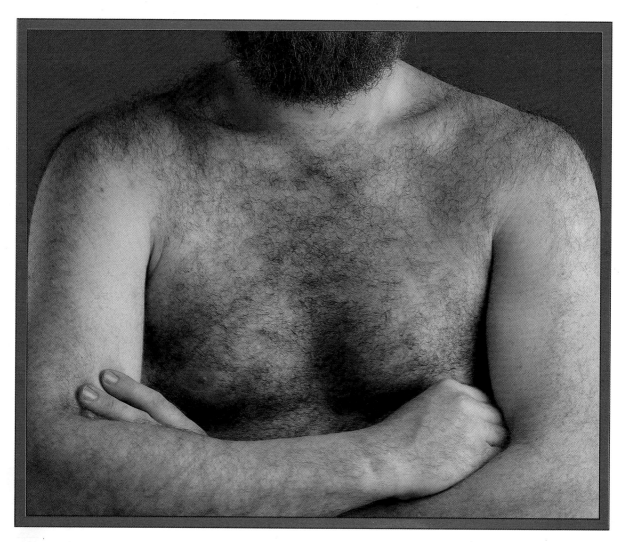

Your whole body, except for
your palms and soles is covered
with fine hair.
Some people have more than others.

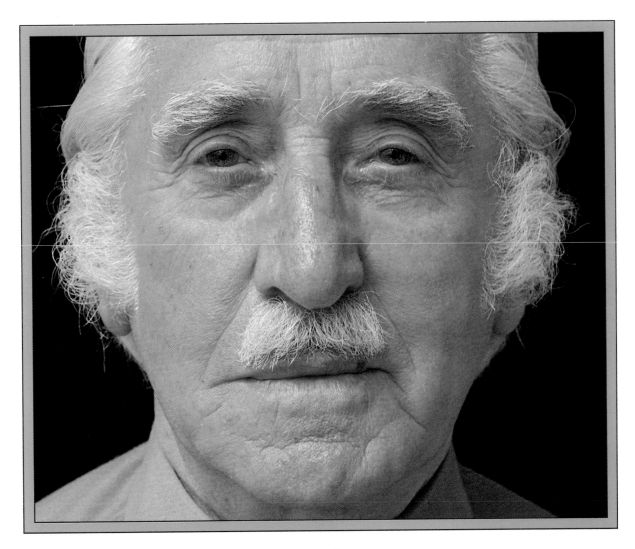

Your eyebrows prevent sweat
from running into your eyes.
Your eyelashes protect your
eyes from specks of dust.

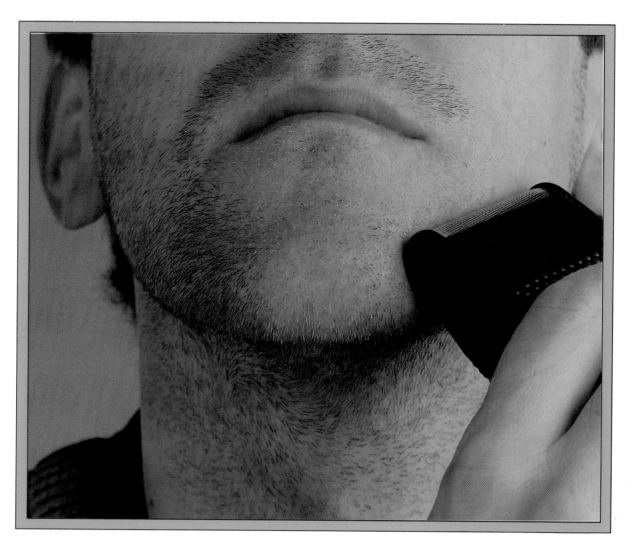

When you grow up, hair will grow
under your arms and between your legs.
Men grow hair on their faces.
Some men shave.

Other men prefer to let their hair
grow into a beard.
This hair is coarser than the hair
on their heads.

What difference would it make
if you had no hair at all?

Do you know?

● On average, a human scalp has 100,000 hairs. Blonde people have about 150,000 hairs, brunettes have about 108,000 hairs and red-heads only about 90,000. Blonde hair grows faster than brown hair.

● Hair is dead! Only the root of the hair (called the follicle) is living. It pushes up the hair cells through the skin.

If you pull out one of your hairs and look at it carefully, you can see the white follicle cells at one end.

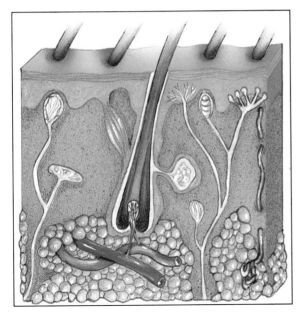

● Each of your hairs has its own lifecycle. Each hair grows without stopping for about 6 years. Then the follicle rests for several months and the hair eventually falls out.

At any one time 10% of your hairs are resting. On average, you lose between 40 and 80 hairs every day.

● The rate at which your hair grows depends upon your age and the state of your health. It grows most quickly after an illness. It grows most slowly in old age, cold weather and during an illness.

On average an adult's hair grows about 1 mm every three days, which is about 13 cm per year.

● Hair is very strong. It can stretch by 25% before it breaks. A single hair can support a weight of 80 grams. If you weighed 80 kilos, you could hang from a cord made from only 1000 of your hairs.

Things to do

● Make a hair survey of your class. Ask your friends to mount one of their hairs on a piece of paper or card. Then arrange them either by length, colour or from straight to curly. Make a block graph of your findings. What is the most common colour of hair? Do more people have straight or curly hair?

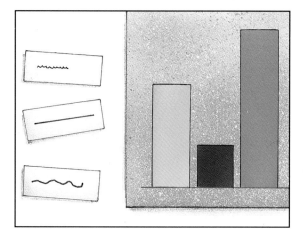

● Make a picture collection of different types of hairstyles. You could collect pictures of hairstyles from countries around the world, or perhaps you might like to make a collection of hairstyles of the past or the present. Write down anything you can find out about them.

● Find out the reasons why members of different religious groups wear their hair in particular ways.

Rastafarians, for example, follow a passage in *The Bible*, which says:

> *'They shall not make baldness upon their head, neither shall they shave off the corner of their beard.'*
> *Leviticus. Ch.21 v.5*

Buddhist monks, on the other hand, shave their heads as a sign of cleanliness and renunciation of the world. What about Sikhs, Christian nuns and monks, Hindus, Moslems and Orthodox Jews?

● Tear up some tissue paper into small pieces. Keep it to hand whilst you brush your hair without stopping for two minutes. When you stop, hold the brush close to your head.

Now brush it again as hard as you can and then hold the brush a few centimetres above the tissue pieces. What do you notice? Find out why this happens.

● Find out how strong your hair is. (You will need a hair at least 8 cm long.) Measure the length of the hair and make a note of it.

Tape one end of the hair to a tabletop and tape a small weight to the other end. Wait five minutes and then measure the hair again. It will have stretched.

Add further weights and measure the hair again. Keep adding weights until the hair snaps.

What weight did it take? How much did it stretch?

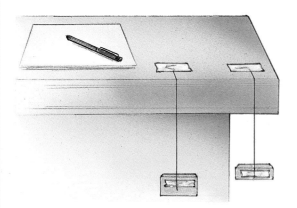

● In the past, wigs were very important and fashionable. Can you find out who wore them and why and how people looked after them? Collect pictures of all sorts of wigs.

Words about hair

The word *hair* is used in many different ways. Can you find out what these words mean?

hair's breadth
hairline
hairpiece
hairshirt
haircloth
hairbrush
haircut
hairstreak
hair-raising
hairdressing

Sayings about hair

These are some sayings about hair. Can you find out what they mean?

To split hairs
To tear one's hair
To make one's hair stand on end
To let one's hair down
To get in one's hair
Not to turn a hair
Keep your hair on!
Got by the short hairs
To make one's hair curl

Index